Moving Your Cars

Nitza Haydee Caro

Published by Nitza Haydee Caro, 2024.

MOVING YOUR CARS

First edition. April 1, 2024.

ISBN: 979-8224575688

Written by Nitza Haydee Caro.

Table of Contents

I want to dedicate this book to my family.

To my husband, Xavier, thank you for being my partner on this journey.

To my kids, Valerie, Jonathan, and Aymara, thank you for making me a better person.

To my granddaughter, Julia, thank you for teaching me so much.

Love you!

Introduction

Life is a game, like a race.

There is only one catch: we have no idea what we are doing.

We only know when our race starts, on the day we are born.

From there, we do not know how long our race will be and what obstacles we will encounter on the way.

Great!

No problem, we can do this. At least everyone gets the same car. Right?

Wait, we all have different cars; that doesn't seem fair. No, it's okay. This race is not a competition, remember. We have different finish lines. So, it doesn't matter what car we have; it is the driver and our skills that matter.

Let's go.

I was not expecting this; the car started multiplying during the race. Now, instead of driving one car, I have duplicate cars named health, career, education, family, friends, money, marriage, and parenthood.

Are we supposed to drive all these cars at the same time? On the same road? And get them all to the finish line?

I don't know about you, but I wouldn't say I like this race.

Who thought this was a good idea?

But everyone is driving, and I don't want to be parked here wondering: How will I do this? So, I will start and see how it goes.

How are you doing?

I have been driving for 46 years, and let me tell you, this race sucks. Don't get me wrong, I've had fun along the way, but whoever designed my road was drunk. Plus, don't we need some rules, maybe a map?

For example, when I married, I thought my husband and I would get in the same car, go in the same direction, and sing karaoke into the sunset. Well, that did not happen. He still has his cars to deal with, and I have mine. We are trying to drive together as best as possible while driving all our cars.

Insane right?

Who would have thought that getting married would multiply your cars? Aren't we consolidating? Nope, we are not.

Then you have the brilliant idea of having kids. If your husband is not in the car, you can have your kids at least. Yes, that will be fun: road trips, snacks, and playing trivia.

Wait a minute; the kids are not in the car with me. They have their cars to drive. So, instead of me driving all of us, I must ensure they know how to drive by themselves and deal with their cars.

My cars are multiplying.

I have my cars, my husband's, and my children's cars, and we are all supposed to ride together.

Can I speak to the game designer?

This race is crazy.

Does anyone have a cheat sheet?

Part 1: Starting the Race

Chapter 1: Accepting your Car

In this race, each person has a different car. Their car comes with a unique set of attributes, skills, and experiences.

The place we are born, family, resources, physical attributes, and mental skills influence the type of race we will drive.

The good news is that each of us has a set of skills that makes us unique, something that is just you. The sad news is that we have difficulty finding out and embracing those skills.

Accepting your car and embracing your journey frees you from baggage.

Welcome to 2024. We have games and lots of them. My personal favorites are the ones where you can choose your character. You can decide your looks, style, and even your name.

In the race of life, it does not work that way. When we are born, everything is already decided for us. We start this race with a specific car chosen just for our journey. Our car does not fit anyone else, is unique, and we are stuck with it until the end of our race. So, why is it so hard for us to accept our car?

I was born and raised in Puerto Rico, which means I am Hispanic, and Spanish is my primary language. I am also an American citizen, and I have learned English in school since kindergarten. Growing up in the Caribbean, I learned to love the heat and the sun, so I don't do well in cold temperatures.

Even though Puerto Ricans come in all colors, shapes, and sizes, I am petite at 5'3". I have curly brown hair and brown eyes, and my skin is white with a light tan. I'm what many would describe as your average Latina.

I did well at school, was a straight-A student, and was Valedictorian at my high school graduation. However, I'm the worst at sports or any physical activity. I can't throw, catch, or hit a ball to save my life. I can't swim, and once, I got an F in physical education because I couldn't ride a bike.

I was born in a traditional middle-class family; my mom and dad met each other when they were teenagers and married young. I was the fourth of five kids, and we were Catholics.

I suffer from motion sickness, which means that even though I like to travel, I have to make sure I take several pills to be able to survive the trip. I have a phobia of lizards, and I'll become a monster when hungry.

On the bright side, I am very good at teaching and always try to be positive. Also, I like to think that I'm funny, even if my family disagrees.

Everything I shared with you has one thing in common: I chose none. It is just who I am, my car.

I'm sure your car is different from mine. That's the idea: we are all one of a kind. We might have some things in common, but no one else is like you.

At first, everyone liked their car. To this day, I haven't heard any babies complaining. However, as we grow up and begin our race, we realize that other people are on the road. We start comparing our cars with theirs; it doesn't improve.

Have you heard the quote that says: "Everyone is a genius. But if you judge a fish by its ability to climb a tree, it will live its whole life believing that it is stupid." As a teacher, this is one of my favorite quotes, which I believe is true. However, we always judge ourselves by how we measure up against everyone else. If we understand that our car is specifically designed for us and our journey, that no two cars or two journeys are the same, then comparing your car to others is a waste of time.

Take twins, for example; even identical twins are different. If you give five bakers the same recipe for a cake, each cake will taste different. To this day, I have never been able to make rice with chicken like my mother made it. Even if I follow every step, it is different.

We all have examples of the same thing. We know this is true; everyone has this unique make-up that no one else can duplicate. Our car is our car; it cannot be returned or exchanged, so we need to learn how to embrace it.

Easier said than done, I know, I have been there. We are used to picking our car apart and making sure everyone knows all the reasons why our car sucks. We are having such a challenging time in our race because of our car. If only our car were different or more like someone else's, I could race much better. How can anyone expect us to have a good race with the car we have?

We are our worst enemies when it comes to judging ourselves. If you have straight hair, you want curly. If you have curly hair, you want straight. If you have short hair, you look at a woman with long hair and think: "If I only knew how to keep my hair like that, I would love to have long hair." The one with long hair thinks: "It takes so long to take care of my hair that if I knew that I could pull a shortcut like her, I would do it in a heartbeat."

If you are a guy, it is not any better. You worry about the hair falling off, bald spots, or getting white hair. You are sure that if your hair looks like Brad Pitt's, all your problems will be solved, but then Jason Statham and Vin Diesel start rocking the bald look, and men everywhere start to wonder if they can pull it off.

Refrain from getting me started on the weight loss business and the never-ending parade of new ways of getting the upgraded you that will finally make you happy. I have been a customer of all these companies all my life, and I have tried everything out there to the point of getting ridiculous. However, even if we know no one can provide a magic solution to our problems, we go back to clicking the one that will work this time.

I know what you are thinking because I have also felt the same. These are superficial problems; I do not care about them. I am talking about the real reason my car sucks: the lack of money and opportunities, my family, and where I live. Why don't you try to have a successful race with those?

I have been there and done that. I'm sure you understand if you grew up with parents who told you: "We can't afford that; money doesn't grow on trees." I always thought: "We don't need a tree; just ask my friend's parents how they get their money; I'm sure it is not from a tree." Then, you become a parent and understand what your parents meant. One time, during my oldest daughter's Girl Scouts meeting, one of the moms asked me where we lived. I told her, and her answer was: "Oh, I know exactly where that is; my maid lives there." Ouch! She said it with a straight face, too. At that moment, I wanted to ask her for one of her money trees.

It takes a while for us to understand that our car can influence but does not determine our race. Yes, I will admit that it is more comfortable to ride in an SUV than a Mini Cooper. However, in the Mini Cooper, you will save gas. Everything has its good and bad points, but at the end of the day, our journey is only ours, and our car is perfect for our trip.

Unfortunately, for us, everything sucks; the car, the trip, and the whole journey is ridiculous. Since we can only experience our journey, we are sure our race is the worst. Our road is the hardest one. We are so sure of it that we spend a lot of our race just trying to convince each other that our race is worse than yours.

For example, I loved my dad; he was the best dad. However, he was an alcoholic, and he smoked since he was 16 years old. As a result of that, he passed away from a heart attack at 47; I was 13 at the time. This part of my race was challenging and guaranteed I would have some tough times down my journey.

Yet, I understand that other cars have had a grimmer time during this race than mine. Yes, my dad was an alcoholic, but he had a job, was an excellent provider for our family, and he was never violent or hit me. I am sure that is not the case for others. Yes, I lost my dad when I was 13, but again, a lot of cars never met their dad. I understand it is easy to fall into the trap of judging and comparing our car's journey to others. Still, it does not change the fact that in my race, during my journey, for my lessons, that was the experience I had to go through. It differs from yours because it is not supposed to be the same.

I am sorry to tell you this, but we cannot control what car we have. The circumstances of our race are not under our control either. That is so hard to accept; it is just not fair. We convince ourselves throughout our race that we can make things happen, that we can make things change, and that we can make it all better. The problem is that everything we want to change is outside our control. We want to ensure that everything will work perfectly and in our favor. We think that if we do the right things, if we make the best decision, if we work harder if we can make people understand our point of view, and if everyone gets along, then all of a sudden, the road will open up, a red carpet will cover our path and our car will hover over it with unicorns shooting rainbows. It does not work that way.

Your life journey will teach you one important lesson:

What is the only thing that we can control?

Ourselves.

What is the only thing we can change?

The way we accept and embrace our race.

What is the only way we can do it?

One day at a time.

Do you want to know how I finally learned this lesson?

Keep reading!

Chapter 2: Balancing Your Cars

During our race, multiple things will happen at the same time. We feel like instead of one car, we are driving multiple cars. Each manages different areas of our lives, and we feel pulled in all directions. Once you realize that your cars multiply constantly, learning how to balance them is essential. If you move one car but forget about the others, eventually, something will go wrong.

Learning how to balance your cars is so hard. We spread ourselves so thin that it is impossible to see a way to do everything all the time and perfectly, too. Now, we cannot see a way because there isn't one. Again, this is something else that we cannot change or control.

There are two main ways that people drive this race. We are either sloths or road runners. If you like fables, you can choose between the turtle and the hare. I am not here to tell you that one is right and the other is wrong. During your race, you can drive however you like.

The sloth or turtles are the ones that take everything at a slow pace. Their goal is to make it to the finish line, slowly and steadily.

The road runners or the hares are the overachievers. Not only will they finish the race with a bang, but it will also be faster and better.

I am sure that right now, you are choosing which one is better or all the reasons why they should or should not act that way. Again, the truth is that it does not matter because it is our race, and it is not a competition.

If you are happy being a sloth, that is good for you. If you are happy being a road runner, then I am so glad for you. Now, are you ready for the catch? What happens when we are not satisfied? What happens when sloths are unhappy because they want more from life? What happens when road runners are never content with their accomplishments?

I am part of the road runners. Again, that is something I did not choose. It is part of my personality. I must be moving and doing things all the time. I could not, even if I tried to take things slow. On top of that, I am a perfectionist. I do not assign a good or bad to that trait because it is a bit of both.

Growing up, I pushed myself to be the best. It was not because my family expected that of me; it was something I wanted to do for myself.

(I want to acknowledge here that some families push many people to achieve and act a certain way, even if that is not what they want, and again, I'm sorry if that is part of your journey.)

During my time in school, I wanted to excel. I didn't accept less than perfect, and that took a toll on my health during my teenage years. I remember my doctor told my mom: "She just needs a couple of Fs in her life, and all her problems will go away."

I was in the choir and youth group at church. I also taught Bible classes to the children after mass. During Christmas, I was involved in the plays and activities. We collected and wrapped toys for the kids. I was also present during Holy Week, back-to-school, Thanksgiving, and summer camp.

Since my dad passed away when I was 13, I started working after school at 14. That was on top of everything else I already told you. I remember the day one of my best friends in college told me, "I've never met anyone who has their life organized every 15 minutes." At that time, I thought that was something to be proud of.

At 18, I felt at the top of my game. Everything was going according to plan. I always said I wanted to get married and have kids fast. So, when I met my husband at 18, the next logical step was to get married. We married when I was 19 and had our first baby when I was 20. I was doing everything right; all my plans aligned, and I was sure my race would be easy.

Can we take a moment here to laugh at my innocence?

That felt good.

Let us continue. My husband is a great man. We have been together for 26 years, have three kids and one granddaughter, and are still going strong. However, it has not been easy.

When I met him, I was dealing with all my cars. I had one for my family. We were dealing with the aftermath of my dad's passing and adjusting to our new reality. Another car was for education; I had to deal with my schoolwork, graduation, college acceptance, and eventually changing majors. I had my work car, which I did part-time after school or on my days off. My friendship car was a big one. I had my school, church, and new college friends all taking a part of my time. I also had my health car, which got much better after high school, but I still had to deal with some things. I had my money car; I had to learn how to manage my money to get the things I needed without burdening my mom.

So, I had my hands full, but I was doing a decent job managing all my cars and ensuring my race was going smoothly. I was sure that once I got married, it would be the same thing; the only change I'd add was my husband. I forgot one little detail: he had his own cars.

My husband is seven years older than me, so by the time I met him, he was 25 years old. He was already divorced and had a daughter. He also had a lot of loans and money baggage, so that car was heavy. He had his family car, work car, friendship car, and health car; you get the idea.

Fast forward 26 years, and now I have a lot of cars to deal with. Our kids also have their cars, and saying it's overwhelming is an understatement. Now, let me make something clear here. I wanted to handle all these cars. I thought it was part of being a wife, a mom, a friend, a family member, and an employee. It is what people do. It is expected from any functional adult who is part of a working society; you must handle your cars. I always thought that because I was a road runner, a perfectionist, and an overachiever, everything was going to be okay. I was sure I could handle everything this race would throw at me.

That was until the day I broke down, and I realized I could not do it anymore. It was all too much; it was too hard. I ran myself into a wall. That is where I understood that I could not control everything, that I could not make things happen, and that it was okay if I were not perfect. I needed to be happy, which meant letting go of control and the idea of perfection. Just like Cas from Clutterbug says: "We don't get bonus points for doing things the hard way."

It is not only essential but imperative that we learn to balance our cars. We are the only ones who decide how we are driving our race. You are the only one in charge of your cars. Let go of the pressure of other people's expectations. Let go of your idea of who we must be for a successful race. Let go of your idea of how many cars we need to have. Perfection is subjective; you will never achieve it because everyone defines it differently, and you cannot make everyone happy.

Success is another word that means different things to everyone. Each person decides what success means to them. It would help if you did not live your life trying to achieve another person's idea of success. We need to choose what cars we will have in our lives, and then we need to balance all of them, putting ourselves first.

I do not want you to reach a breaking point to understand finally:

What is the only thing that we can control?

Ourselves.

What is the only thing we can change?

The way we accept and embrace our race.

What is the only way we can do it?

One day at a time.

What do we need to keep our sanity throughout this race?

We need to balance our cars and put ourselves first.

I had to learn another lesson to balance my cars and finally put myself first. I will tell you, keep reading!

Chapter 3: Good Drivers, Bad Drivers

No one said that all the drivers we encounter on our roads will be good. One of the lessons we must learn is that sometimes people are just bad drivers, and the only reason they are there is to teach you.

We are on the road, driving our cars, and trying to do an excellent job. We start looking around and seeing other cars there, and we believe they are also trying to do a decent job. We are all there in the race of life, trying to be our best selves, and we start smiling because life is good, and those cars have our best interests at heart. We are all human. We are all in this together. Suddenly, one of those cars hit us on the side of our car. They want to get us out of their way. We are stunned. How can that be? There must be a mistake.

Growing up, everyone taught us to be friendly, and everyone needed to get along. We are all friends here. Then, one day, during recess, we were playing, and during a race, another kid pushed us, and we scraped our knees. The teacher comes running and says: "It was an accident. He or she did not mean it." Then they turned around and said to the kid: "Say you are sorry." The kid will say: "Sorry." We find ourselves saying: "It's okay." But the truth is, the kid was not sorry, and it was not okay.

If you grew up as I did in the church, you were taught since childhood that everyone is good at heart. We are all children of God and need to help one another. We learn to approach everyone with the idea that they are good. They will be kind to us if we are kind to them. That if we help them, they will help us. If the person acts incorrectly, it is because they are going through a tough time or having a difficult day. My favorite part was when they turned the whole thing around and asked: "What did you do if they acted that way? You must have done something to upset them."

Since we want to be good drivers and believe that everyone is good at heart, we drive down our road without guarding our hearts. We are an open book. We want to help people. We want to make things better. We wear our hearts on our sleeves. We believe that people will never hurt us on purpose. Sadly, as we keep racing down the road, driving our cars, we encounter more situations that challenge those ideas.

I will be careful in writing this next point because I know it will ruffle some feathers. I understand that what I consider or refer to in this chapter as bad drivers might be just drivers that have a mental disorder and that their condition is part of their cars. People who suffer from narcissism, antisocial personality disorder, addiction, pathological lying, borderline personality disorder, or sexual predators, to name a few, might not be able to control those traits. They might need to recognize their problem, be willing to get help and stick with the treatment to improve. However, we know that it is easier said than done, and most of these drivers are convinced they are fine and everybody else is the problem.

Considering our first lesson, that the only thing we can control is ourselves, puts us in a tricky situation when we encounter this type of driver on the road. Why? Because we are fighting between the belief that everyone is good at heart and we want to help them be better, and the fact that we cannot change anyone but ourselves.

At that moment, we encounter "the good" driver problem. We make ourselves the target of those bad drivers. I once heard that our race would be so much easier if our cars were like NASCAR cars, with all the stickers around letting us know who we are. Imagine how much easier it would be if you see a car approaching you on the road and you see the sticker that says: "compulsive liar." Wow! That would be so much easier. We could push our gas pedal and get as far away from that car as possible. If we do not have another choice, let us say it is a coworker. You can nod and smile while thinking: "I see you; I do not believe a word you are saying right now."

Sadly, life's race is not like that. We do not get a cheat sheet. We must learn as we drive. That means falling for lies or manipulation. It sucks big time. Again, I want to ensure you understand that I am not saying bad drivers should not be on the road. It is their race, too, and they are learning from their race as much as we are from ours. Many of those drivers we encounter have a reason to be there and a lesson to teach us. It might hurt, put a dent in us for the rest of our race, and almost take us off the road entirely, but if you are strong enough to survive the lesson, you become a better driver.

When we become better drivers, learn our lessons, and survive that part of our road, we understand that we have the right to choose who rides alongside us on our journey. It is a hard lesson to learn, but one that changes our life forever. We understand that those bad drivers could be our parents, our siblings, our family, our friends, our coworkers, our partners, and yes, even our children. We allow ourselves to say NO when we realize it is our race and we are the only car we can control. We will be the same beautiful, kind, good driver that we were before. We understand that we do not have to be the bumper car everyone hits in our race. We are in control of our car, and we are strong.

This lesson will go against everything we were taught like only selfish drivers put themselves first and have boundaries. Excellent and kind drivers are always looking out for everyone else's cars, not anymore. Now we know those terrible drivers are not our concern; it is not our job to drive their cars, which do not belong in our journey.

So, the next time we face a bad driver, remember:

What is the only thing that we can control?

Ourselves.

What is the only thing we can change?

The way we accept and embrace our race.

What is the only way we can do it?

One day at a time.

What do we need to keep our sanity throughout this race?

We need to balance our cars and put ourselves first.

How do we put ourselves first?

By taking bad drivers out of our journey.

Now that we have learned these lessons, we are ready. The road is ahead, and our journey is waiting for us. Are we feeling more confident in our driving skills? Can we face the obstacles on the road?

Let my lessons help you understand these challenging driving conditions. Keep reading!

Part 2: The Obstacles on the Road

Chapter 4: Detours

Let us be honest: as much as we want to put our car in cruise control from the beginning of our race to the end, obstacles will force us to slow down. One of these obstacles is the detours on the road. Most detours we will face are unexpected and can change our lives forever.

We are driving down the road. It is a beautiful day, and we are happy because everything is working out. Our race is going smoothly, and things are under control, or that is what we thought. Suddenly, we see it, a detour up ahead, and without us having any say on the matter, our familiar road changes. Now, we are facing a new road with many unknowns, and we cannot help but wonder why.

Remember when I told you I got married at 19? I was in my 3rd year of college and working part-time then. I moved to my husband's town, so I was now driving 45 minutes to get to school when I lived within walking distance. It was an adjustment, and more than once, I fell asleep in class because I was exhausted. Yes, I was happy, but adding a whole new bunch of cars was a challenge. However, I am a road runner. So, of course, the smart thing to do in that situation is to have a baby.

We were married for three months when I got pregnant. It was not an accident; we discussed it and had everything figured out. My husband was a truck driver, and I was doing well at college while working part-time. I would have the baby during the summer before starting my senior year, and my mom was more than happy to babysit her first granddaughter. We checked all our boxes, and everyone was happy and excited.

Ready for the detour? My husband lost his job. The truckers went on strike, and the company decided to fire them all. Great, we had a newborn and no job. I was not working at the time because I was on maternity leave. Our race suddenly stopped, and we needed a new plan. My husband got a job offer in Florida, and after talking about it, he decided to take it.

That is what I call a detour; I went from having all my life figured out to starting over in a new country. I was 20 years old with a 3-month-old baby and was all alone for the first time in my life. We left all our family and friends behind. I dropped out of college and became a stay-at-home mom. My husband worked 14 hours a day, six days a week, and we only had one car. On Sundays, we went to the supermarket and ensured we had everything we needed for the week. We lived in a 1-bedroom apartment with nothing within walking distance. I was in the apartment with nothing to do during the week. I was miserable and depressed. Why? I asked myself all the time. I had everything figured out. I did everything right.

We can all think about one or multiple detours in our lives. Those moments when life puts an exit on the road, and we need to make a decision that changes the direction of our journey. Sometimes, you are forced to make that detour, like when a spouse asks you for a divorce. Other times, your actions and decisions can change the road. It is easy to fall down the rabbit hole of asking why, of feeling sorry for ourselves. Somehow, it is hard for us to understand that every decision has a consequence. It is even harder to accept that other people's decisions can also bring consequences to your race. That feeling of being unable to control our lives or our future, knowing everything can change in the blink of an eye, is hard to swallow.

However, once you embrace those changes, a whole new world of possibilities opens before you. It took me one year to understand that I had to stop my pity party and make new plans for our new life. I stopped looking at what I had left behind and started to list all the new options I had in front of me. After that, I went for it. I knew I still had a lot of life before me, and the probability of having more detours in our lives was high. Nonetheless, I knew I could do it if I could look at the detours on my road as new possibilities.

Because in our race, we need to remember:
What is the only thing that we can control?
Ourselves.
What is the only thing we can change?
The way we accept and embrace our race.
What is the only way we can do it?
One day at a time.
What do we need to keep our sanity throughout this race?

We need to balance our cars and put ourselves first.

How do we put ourselves first?

By taking bad drivers out of our journey.

How can we accept the detours on our road?

By looking at them as new possibilities.

I will admit that the potential of facing detours on our road is scary, but having accidents on your road takes things to a whole new level.

If you want to know about this lesson, keep reading!

Chapter 5: Accidents on the Road

Even the best drivers can get into accidents.

Why?

Because you cannot control everyone's cars, even if you take all the precautions, safety measures, and classes, you can still get into an accident.

Sometimes, it is your fault because you make a mistake despite all your efforts.

We are human, remember!

Other times, it is not your fault, and you watch yourself crashing without any control of the situation. You can only embrace yourself for the impact.

It's another day when you find yourself in your car on your way home. You are tired after a long day at work and cannot wait to get some rest. The afternoon traffic is heavier than usual, and then you realize something is wrong. You hear sirens, and now you know there has been an accident, and you have no idea how long you will have to wait. Even though you are angry at the situation and the long wait, you might think that the people involved in the accident are having a worse day than you are. Nobody likes to be involved in an accident; sometimes, it can change your life forever.

In the race of life, we also encounter accidents that can alter our journey. Sometimes, our accidents are temporary inconveniences, or they can be significant life-changing events. In my case, our accident was an actual accident, and it created a ripple effect that lasted five years.

It was 2006; we have been married for nine years. We had our 8-year-old daughter and our 3-year-old son. After the death of my mom to cancer, which was a hard lesson on my race, and losing our mobile home to a hurricane, it was not a fun experience either. We were back on track and feeling happy after buying our second home, a brand-new house in a new development. We could choose the plot of land we wanted and the design of the house. We picked everything, from the tiles to the kitchen and bathrooms; it was our dream home. We moved in, and six months later, in December 2006, my husband had an accident on his truck.

My husband drove double trailers, and while stopped at a red light, another truck driver hit him from behind. He was not paying attention, so he did not notice that the light was red. You can imagine the impact; it was not a car but another truck. My husband wasn't moving; he was waiting for the green light. The fact that he had two trailers hooked to his truck made the wave of the impact harder. I thank God every day that he was okay and that he didn't have to go to the hospital. However, after things got worse, we realized he had three herniated disks, he had damaged his neck, and he had bursitis in his right shoulder. Can you give us a break? I mean, come on, we just went through a lot, and now this.

It took one year after the accident for my husband to go back to work. Even when he went back, the pain was terrible, and a couple of times, when he would try to bend down to get something, he would get stuck and could not get back up. It was a terrifying situation. He had to stop working and give his back enough time to heal, or he could end up paralyzed. He was just 36 years old, and it was his turn to get into a depression.

The only way we could give him enough time to heal was to move back to Puerto Rico, so we did. It was 2009. I had just graduated with my bachelor's degree, and I could keep things going while he got better. However, we lost everything. We lost our house, we lost our business, and we had to file for bankruptcy. This experience was an extremely hard part of our journey for all of us. My husband was still young but felt like he could not provide for our family anymore. Our kids had to get used to an unfamiliar environment and schools. They speak Spanish and frequently traveled to Puerto Rico on vacation, but the change was still hard on them. Plus, I was not dealing with the situation any better, watching everything we worked so hard to build crumble down.

It took two years for us to decide to move back to Florida. My husband was feeling much better, and after calling his old boss, he got his job back. My kids were ready to return, and I was, too. I had an excellent job and a lot of friends, but I had to do what was best for all of us, and that was to move back. We had to start from the beginning with only one car and almost no furniture, but we did it and were able to build everything back up. It took a lot of time. It took work. In 2016, we bought our third home precisely ten years after our second home and one year after having our 3rd child, which is a story for another time.

No one wants to be involved in an accident. It's even more frustrating when you feel like it was not your fault, and now you have to go through all the problems and setbacks. However, like with everything else on our journey, each accident we have during our race teaches us a lesson. Please do not be mad at me. I know it is not easy to accept; it is hard, but it is still the truth. Now, when we look back at everything that happened, I thank God for seeing us through it, and I would not change any of it. Yes, it was a hard lesson to go through. At the same time, it made our family stronger. Our marriage is better because we went through all of this together. Now, we appreciate everything more because we know how hard it was to fight for it. At the same time, now we know that even if we lose everything again, it is not the end of the world, and we can make it.

SO, WHEN YOU ARE GOING through an accident in your life, remember:

What is the only thing that we can control?

Ourselves.

What is the only thing we can change?

The way we accept and embrace our race.

What is the only way we can do it?

One day at a time.

What do we need to keep our sanity throughout this race?

We need to balance our cars and put ourselves first.

How do we put ourselves first?

By taking bad drivers out of our journey.

How can we accept the detours on our road?

Looking at them as new possibilities.

How can we recover from our accidents?

Knowing that they make us stronger.

Once you go through an accident that shakes your life, you think that nothing can take you down anymore. This race will prove otherwise to you.

Keep reading if you want to know about the lesson that almost took me down!

Chapter 6: The Tornado on the Road

These types of storms are unpredictable, and it is hard to prepare for them. Even with the best intentions and carefully laid out plans, you can't do much when life throws a tornado in your path.
You hold on tight, hope you can make it to the other side, and then try to rebuild everything with what is left behind.
The other thing is that even if a twister in your road does not last very long when you are in it, you feel like it's never going to end.

"Things go wrong. You can't explain it; you can't predict it." Movie-Twister (1996).

If you saw the movie Twister, I am sure you thought more than once, what would you do if you encountered that type of storm on the road? With car cameras and cell phones, we have seen live videos where cars get pulled into these wind vortices. Whenever I see one of these videos, I think about the people in the car. How are they feeling? What are they thinking at that moment? I hold my breath, hoping they will be okay.

In the race of life, we could encounter one of these storms. If you thought the detours and accidents on the road could test you, the tornado on the road has the power to destroy you. I faced one of these storms, and it almost took me down. However, I survived, which is why I am writing this book. I want to let you know that you can survive it, too.

As parents, we can withstand any challenge that we face. We find ourselves with the strength to handle anything. One of my favorite quotes is: "You never know how strong you are until being strong is your only choice." We have all seen videos of mothers getting cars off their kids. The adrenaline of the moment gives them the strength to do whatever it takes to save them. Other times, the strength is not physical but emotional and mental.

In some cases, they might have a happy ending. However, what happens when you realize that you do not have the control to stop things from happening? What happens when, despite your best efforts, things go wrong?

"I can't wait for my kids to grow up." This comment is something I am sure we have heard and said to ourselves more than once. As your kids grow up, you realize the error of that statement, and you can only smile and nod when you hear a younger parent say the same thing. The truth is that when your kids are little, it is the best time of your parenthood experience. Why? Because you know what they are doing and ensure their environment and friends are safe. When they start to grow up, all that goes out the window. I can hear you now saying: "You just need to teach them right from wrong and trust that they will make the right decisions." Well, that does not work either.

Sometimes, they will choose the right thing to do, but eventually, they will mess up—some more than others—and we can do nothing about it. We have done it ourselves, and thinking our kids will not make mistakes is not an accurate expectation.

This realization was a hard pill for me to swallow. I wanted to be the best mom. Of course, I knew everything my mom did wrong and would make sure I did not do the same. For that reason, I read all the books, saw all the videos, and did all my research to give my children all the opportunities for them to succeed. In other words, their cars were ready to go, and they had all the knowledge to have the best race and a good journey. That only lasted until high school graduation. They turned 18, and all the bets were off.

My oldest daughter was 20 when she met someone and decided to get married. Even though my husband and I knew it was not the right decision, we could not do anything about it. As time passed, I told her she should wait for a baby. We knew things were not as great as she was trying to let us think, and she was not happy, but of course, it was not our decision either. She was married for 2 ½ years when they decided to have a baby, and she got pregnant immediately. During her 5th month of pregnancy, her husband asked for a divorce. It was at that moment, when she was having an accident during her journey, that she let me know that everything was my fault.

My son was not doing much better. He joined the Army before he graduated high school and was off to basic training in July after graduation. The Army was his dream, and all his plans revolved around having a military career. Like his dad, he has a weakness for cars, and during this time, he did not make the best decisions or deals, which cost him and us a lot of money. His track record with women could have been better, too. These relationships cost him a lot of money, a couple of accidents, and ended up ruining his credit. All this happened during his two years of service. In March 2022, he was discharged from the military (together with many other service members), and again, during this detour in his life, he found himself back home.

During this time, I would see them struggle with everything that was happening, and I kept blaming myself. When you have both kids coming back home after trying life and failing, it is easy to try to go back and find where I went wrong. I would think: "I wasted my life." All this time, my only job was to be a good mom, and what does it say about me that both my kids were unsuccessful? Even worse, how do I continue raising my youngest child when now I would second guess everything and fear it will not work again? It took me a while to understand that they did not fail; it was just a part of their journey. They had to go through the experience to learn one of many lessons they would encounter on the road. As a mom, I did not fail either, even if that part took me longer to learn.

If you think your accidents on the road are bad, try to witness your kids' accidents. I've had a good marriage; having to go through a divorce process with my daughter is so much worse. I was helping her cope with the reality of being a single mother, not something that I wanted for her either. Trying to help my son rebuild his career path and credit is a challenging experience. Saying that everyone in our house had difficulty adjusting to new paths on our journeys for two years is an understatement.

Then it happened: the tornado on the road. I received a phone call from my daughter that would change our lives forever. My 10-month-old granddaughter was in the hospital. She received a message from the baby's father saying that the baby was having seizures; she was leaving work and heading straight to the emergency room. We spent seven weeks (about one and a half months) with my granddaughter in the hospital. We almost lost her, and the fact that we can still have her with us is a miracle. However, she now has permanent neurological damage, and we have no idea what her prognosis is going to be.

At that moment, during those weeks, I saw what was left of my family crumble. My husband, who has always been strong, has completely broken down. Seeing our granddaughter fighting for her life on that bed in the PICU was an experience that changed him forever. The amount of anger and hate radiating from him is something I have never seen and that I wish I did not see again. All the whys were running through his head, and he wondered what he could have done to prevent it.

My daughter was moving on autopilot. I cannot even imagine her despair at the possibility of losing her daughter and, at the same time, feeling guilty because, despite all her best efforts, she could not protect her. Even now, without definite answers and no prognosis on site, the fear of the unknown and how she is going to handle all of this by herself is overwhelming.

My son has always been the silent one. He suffers quietly and thinks that he must be strong for everyone else. As his mom, I knew what he was feeling and thinking. I needed to make sure he got an outlet for that anger before it could cause more damage.

My little one, so full of love, kept an optimistic attitude throughout the ordeal. It is not an easy task to explain to an eight-year-old that her niece might be dying. At first, she was confused and had so many questions. The same ones we had, and sadly, we did not have the answers. Those first five days took a toll on us; she was no exception. One of those nights when we were praying, she said: "I don't think Jesus loves me anymore because he is not listening to my prayer." Talk about a shot right to your heart. Thankfully, Jesus was listening to her prayers, and the next day, we had news that the baby's brain activity was back.

I cannot even begin to describe to you the amount of anger, frustration, and feeling of helplessness that I went through during that time. Our family, who had been through so much, was unprepared for this storm. It took me a lot of time and tears to understand that I cannot control everything. I could not do it even if my instinct were to get in there and fix everything for everyone. It was not in my hands. We spend months asking, fighting, and looking for answers, only to have people tell us: "You have to let it go."

At that moment, I was not ready to hear those words. Eventually, I had to accept that I had to let it go because it was not in my hands. We had a lot of people involved in this situation, each of us driving through our race at the same time, and even if their race and their journey were causing me a lot of grief, I had to let things play out.

At this time in my life, I finally understood that I was not responsible for other people's choices and that even if they were my kids, they needed to learn by themselves. I knew that I had to let go and let each of them learn their lessons because they are not the same for everyone, and by trying to save them from the lesson, I was not doing them any favors.

I took this type of storm in my life to finally understand:

What is the only thing that we can control?

Ourselves.

What is the only thing we can change?

The way we accept and embrace our race.

What is the only way we can do it?

One day at a time.

What do we need to keep our sanity throughout this race?

We need to balance our cars and put ourselves first.

How do we put ourselves first?

By taking bad drivers out of our journey.

How can we accept the detours on our road?

Looking at them as new possibilities.

How can we recover from our accidents?

Knowing that they make us stronger.

How do you survive a tornado on your road?

Learning to let go.

I am sure you can tell me about the tornado in your life. If you have not gone through one yet, I am happy for you and hope you do not have to. However, I learned something important by facing all those obstacles in my life. I must take care of myself.

If you want to know what happened to me to learn that lesson, keep reading!

Part 3: Taking Care of Your Car

Chapter 7: Stop for Gas

Why do we need gas?

Because our cars cannot run without it.

However, we race through life without caring for ourselves or refueling our tanks. Our need to refuel is physical, mental, and spiritual.

The saying, "You can't give what you don't have," is repeated often. "You need to take better care of yourself." This beautiful sentiment is profound yet difficult to follow.

We feel guilty if we take time to refuel ourselves, but someone has to say this: "Hey, you, the one running with the needle on the E on the gas tank. If you do not refuel, you will stop in the middle of the road. You will cause traffic jams, accidents and force detours for many people."

So, by stopping for gas, you are doing a public service.

Are you in the group that thinks they need to refuel their cars when the needle is on the half tank, or are you one of the daredevils who likes to run with the gas light turned on because you want to live on the edge? Either way, we need to add gas to our cars regularly to be able to use them, even if the gas price makes you wish they would run on water.

During our race of life, we need to add gas to our cars, too. We must take care of ourselves to drive, but it is hard because we are taught from an early age not to be selfish. Any self-care is seen by many as selfish and is frowned upon. Especially if you are a mom, you are expected to put everyone's needs ahead of yours. We know we need a break, and time to ourselves is required but rarely taken. We are good at pushing ourselves, sometimes beyond what is healthy. When your family needs you, it is easy to forget about yourself.

While my mom was sick, I had to stay with her for four months in Puerto Rico. My husband remained in Florida. During that time, my oldest kids were 7 and 2, and my younger brother was still living at home while attending college. It was hard to take care of everyone and, at the same time, bring my mom to her cancer treatments and doctor's appointments. I lost a lot of weight and barely slept, but at 27 years old, I could do it without burning myself out.

However, when my granddaughter was in the hospital, I was 45, and believe me, it is not the same. Something will give when you try to be everything to everyone and put yourself through that amount of stress. This time, it took just two months before I found myself in the back of an ambulance. When I got to the hospital and talked to the doctor, he asked: "Have you been stressed lately? Having trouble sleeping? How about your diet? Are you eating?" Well, that was three for three, and I am out. I was running with my gas tank empty. At that time, I was not doing anyone a favor by running myself into a wall. The last thing we needed was for me to get sick.

While your physical health is essential, you must also take care of your spiritual and mental health; this is also part of putting gas in your car. We are not machines, and the number of things we want to accomplish in one day is impossible. Our minds cannot handle so much stress. We must be kind to ourselves because even if we push ourselves to the limit, eventually, we will run out of gas.

Stop and think: "Who are we trying to impress? Do we think we are indispensable and no one else can do what we do? Will we get an award for being the most indispensable person ever? Do we want recognition or appreciation? Is it our responsibility to run everything and ensure everyone is all right? Are we trying to fulfill someone else's idea of how you should act? Do we want to solve world hunger and bring world peace simultaneously?

I decided to love myself first because I love my family. It's not healthy to carry the world's weight on my shoulders. That meant giving up the idea of perfection and trusting each person to do what they must do for themselves, even if they do not do things the same way as me. Even if they make mistakes along the way, I would love them through it but respect them enough to understand it is their journey. It sounds simple and logical, but it takes work to do. However, if I did it, you can do it too.

Do not wait until you are in the hospital to understand:

What is the only thing that we can control?

Ourselves.

What is the only thing we can change?

The way we accept and embrace our race.

What is the only way we can do it?

One day at a time.

What do we need to keep our sanity throughout this race?

We need to balance our cars and put ourselves first.

How do we put ourselves first?

By taking bad drivers out of our journey.

How can we accept the detours on our road?

Looking at them as new possibilities.

How can we recover from our accidents?

Knowing that they make us stronger.

How do you survive a tornado on your road?

Learning to let go.

How do we take care of our car?

By taking care of ourselves.

Taking care of your car might be more work than you thought. "It takes a village," right? So, it would help if you had your team lined up.

Let me tell you about my village and everyone who came to my rescue; keep reading!

Chapter 8: Pit Stop

Your car needs help; all the dash lights are on, the wheels are on the rims, and smoke is coming out of who knows where.
You need to make an emergency stop and try to get your team of people to help you.

Going down the road, you feel your car acting weird. A strange noise is coming from somewhere in the front. Suddenly, the lights on the dashboard come to life, and the car dies. If you are anything like me, you have no idea what is happening or how to fix it. Nonetheless, you open the hood of the car and look inside, hoping you see a sign there that tells you precisely what is wrong and how to fix it. But since your car is not helpful, you know it is time to call reinforcements.

During the race of life, our car will find itself in different situations you will have no idea how to fix. You know by now that you need to take care of your car and that you need to stop for gas; this is something you can do by yourself, even if you wait until the last minute to do it. Other times, the car will need more specialized equipment and maintenance. That is when you need to have your Pit Stop Crew.

Each of our teams is going to look different. Remember that there is no one-size-fits-all formula for anything in this race. Your car and your journey are unique, so it is only logical that your crew is unique, too. You might have your partner as part of your crew, some family members, friends who can be part of your team, spiritual guides, or even therapists. This squad can and should change as your race progresses. Just as this quote says: "People come into your life for a reason, a season, or a lifetime." By now, you should know I love quotes, right? There is something valuable about these nuggets of wisdom that have withstood the test of time.

Anyway, let us continue with our pit crew. You choose these groups of people, or they can be as random as someone you meet on the street. They provide you with what you need at the right time. For example, when my granddaughter was fighting for her life, multiple groups from various parts of our lives answered the call for prayers. It was a humbling experience to know how many people had our baby and family in their prayers. People added her name to prayer chains worldwide for five days, and we witnessed a miracle together. I did not call for those prayers; my crew did, and I will be forever grateful.

Of course, your mom, brother, best friend, or pastor can be part of your crew. In challenging parts of your journey, you might need the assistance of a therapist or psychologist who can help you work through a rough time. Other times, it might be someone who has a message for you. I remember one day, I was working when I found out about my daughter's divorce and my son's discharge. Both things happened at the same time, and I was struggling. One customer, a lovely lady in her 80s, came to the office. She looked at me and asked me if I was okay. I told her I was fine; I had issues with my kids. She never asked me what the problem was; she just told me about her two sons and her struggles with them. At the end, she said: "Take care of yourself and your marriage. Your kids will figure it out. You already taught them what they needed to know; now it is their time to put it to the test." I thanked her and told her she was sent to give me that message that day. I needed to hear it, even if it took me some time to accept. But she was right, and for the time of that conversation, she was part of my crew.

Do not let pride keep you from asking for help when needed. This race is tough, and knowing when you are in over your head is important. Also, feel free to fire some crew members if they are sabotaging your car. My daughter was heartbroken when she learned one of her most trusted crew members was betraying her by sharing confidential information; those lessons are hard to understand but necessary.

Get yourself surrounded by a pit crew that can help you understand:
What is the only thing that we can control?
Ourselves.
What is the only thing we can change?
The way we accept and embrace our race.
What is the only way we can do it?
One day at a time.
What do we need to keep our sanity throughout this race?
We need to balance our cars and put ourselves first.
How do we put ourselves first?

By taking bad drivers out of our journey.

How can we accept the detours on our road?

Looking at them as new possibilities.

How can we recover from our accidents?

Knowing that they make us stronger.

How do you survive a tornado on your road?

Learning to let go.

How do we take care of our car?

By taking care of ourselves.

Why do you need the best Pit Crew?

Because everyone needs reinforcements.

I love my Pit Crew and hope you have an incredible team around you. Now, even if you have great support, how do you know when to ask for help, and what is the one thing you must learn that will change your race?

Want to find out? Keep reading!

Chapter 9: The Owner's Manual

We all know the book in the glove compartment—the one that we ignore and never open. It is supposed to teach us everything about our car.

In the race of life, we do not get an owner's manual; you need to write it yourself. Getting to know yourself is the only way to find out what to put in there. That way, you understand how to drive your race more efficiently. Also, you learn when something is wrong and you need to ask for help.

Modern cars are complicated machines built with hundreds of pieces that allow you to have a secure and comfortable vehicle to travel. Each part is essential for the car to work. I admit my knowledge about cars is zero. However, my husband loves cars, and I have been there with him multiple times while he tries to figure out what is wrong with them. After a lot of fighting, it turns out it was a fuse or a loose screw. Other times, it could be an electrical problem or a part that needs to be changed. I appreciate his knowledge about cars and the amount of money we save by him doing the basic work that is necessary to keep our cars working correctly. At the same time, I understand that if he didn't know about cars or I was alone, I wouldn't know how to fix what was broken. Of course, I can always learn, which is this chapter's point.

Since we do not get an owner's manual at the beginning of our race, we are stuck with our car and must figure out how to take care of it. Of course, we initially rely on our parents and family to keep us safe and healthy. They learn how to understand the different cries and tantrums to know how you feel or what you want. At the same time, you learn their idea of how to take care of your car by how they learned to take care of their car. However, each car is unique, and even though some general aspects can apply to every car, it is our job to find out what makes our car work and what makes it stop.

I know that some cars choose to keep crying and throwing tantrums all their race in the hope that everyone else will know what they need and fix it or even drive their race for them. At the same time, other cars decide to drive the race without really getting too deep into what can improve their journey. To each their own, and if that is how they want to drive their race, I support them 100%.

However, if you are reading this book, I hope you are part of the group that realizes there must be a better way to do this than what you have been doing so far. I also hope that with my journey, I can help you get some pointers to improve your race. Here is one of those clues you need to learn about yourself.

You are special and one of a kind. Your journey is also all about you. So, I am not here to tell you exactly how to drive your race. Instead, you should know that it is your privilege to learn about your car and what works for you all by yourself. Of course, we can consider everything we are taught, and then we get to decide what applies to us and what does not. For example, let us take the belief that you should sleep 8 hours per night. I know people that will make sure they sleep 8 hours. The other group will tell you they need to sleep 5 hours and are ready to go. On the other hand, you know another group that needs to sleep at least 10 hours before they can feel human. Each one of those people is correct. Why? Because they know their cars and know what works for them. Again, if we try to impose a specific time for everybody, it will not work because we are all different. How many people do you know like to work nights because that's when they feel more productive? Another group, the early risers, hit the ground running before sunrise.

You might consider this a silly example, but the premise is the same and works in every decision you make. We can think about everything you have learned and decide what works for you. Now, the illogical thing we always do is believe that our argument about our preference will make any difference in how other people make their decisions. Nonetheless, we spend hours of our race trying to do just that. I know because I was one of them. It wasn't until I finally understood that I could do what I wanted, you could do what you wanted, and we could still all drive our cars and go about our journey that I finally felt a huge weight lifted from my shoulders.

You must learn what works for you and use that knowledge to drive your best race. It does not matter how other people drive their cars; you cannot change them. I can hear all of you saying: "What do you mean it does not matter how other people drive their race? If the way they do it affects me, I have the right to complain. I must let them know they are messing with my journey." Now, are you ready for this? I will let you know what fixed that problem for me, and it changed my race: evasive maneuvers.

What? Evasive maneuvers? Yep, you need to take control of your car and think you are part of the movie Fast and Furious. Whenever you see someone or something on the road that can affect your race, go right, go left, or drive in reverse if you must. You must make sure that at the end of the day, we can say like MC Hammer: "You can't touch this," and have fun with it at the same time. This race is a game. Remember, you do not have to engage if people are out to get you, even if they are out for a fight or want to involve you in their drama. If they intend to use you as their butler, channel your inner Vin Diesel or Michelle Rodriguez, hit that nitrous, and say: "See ya."

It feels so good to learn and take control of your car. When you do, it will be easy to understand:

What is the only thing that we can control?

Ourselves.

What is the only thing we can change?

The way we accept and embrace our race.

What is the only way we can do it?

One day at a time.

What do we need to keep our sanity throughout this race?

We need to balance our cars and put ourselves first.

How do we put ourselves first?

By taking bad drivers out of our journey.

How can we accept the detours on our road?

Looking at them as new possibilities.

How can we recover from our accidents?

Knowing that they make us stronger.

How do you survive a tornado on your road?

Learning to let go.

How do we take care of our car?

By taking care of ourselves.

Why do you need the best Pit Crew?

Because everyone needs reinforcements.

How do you learn to control your car?

By learning those evasive maneuvers.

By now, we should know all the tools needed for a successful race. However, there is one more part that we need to address. One that makes the race challenging because it is something so hard to ignore.

If you want to know what it is, keep reading!

Part 4: The Distractions on the Road

Chapter 10: Stop Pushing Other People's Cars

"Why don't you just do it?"
"Can't you see it is for your own good?"
Again, we are all guilty of this. No matter how bad our lives are going, we always know what someone else needs to do to solve their problems. It is a hobby really that makes us 1,000 times better than Dr. Phil, hands down.

We are all guilty of this. You are on the road, and the car in front of you is not moving or going too slow. You want to scream in frustration, honk the horn, and somehow let them know they are in your way. We have been in both spots in this scenario, and I am sure we can all agree that the more someone pushes, the more you are going to die there to make them squirm. You can admit it; we have all done it. The funny thing is that when it is our turn to push, we still do it no matter what.

Nagging, demanding, critical, overbearing, and preachy are some words we can all use to describe all the people in our lives who provided unsolicited advice. At the same time, these are the words other people use to describe us when we provide unsolicited advice. What makes us think that if we hate it when someone tells us what to do or how to live our lives, other people will appreciate us doing it to them?

It's often difficult to break the habit of gossiping. From a young age, we're exposed to hearing our family, friends, and colleagues talk about others or the latest news. Gossiping is a common source of entertainment for many people. We enjoy listening to stories and giving our own opinions about other people's lives. If given the chance, we may even offer our advice to those involved in the situation.

We can be vicious of one another. You can read a comment thread on social media to understand the lengths people go to make their opinions heard and ensure everyone knows it is correct. Before the internet, you might have to endure a lecture from your well-meaning neighbor. Now, after the internet, you have someone from another country telling you why you are an idiot and will single-handedly be the cause of the end of the world. Whoa! Can we chill for a moment?

If you are in the race, driving your car, keep your eyes on the road. Every time you stop paying attention to your journey to see who Taylor Swift's new boyfriend is, you might lose momentum in your race. Whenever you call your sister to tell her that you saw your nephew looking at some magazines and it might be time to schedule an intervention, you are taking attention off your road.

Here is another of my favorite quotes: "The road to hell is paved with good intentions." Some examples of this are when you receive a backhanded compliment, when someone gives you advice, or when someone tells you something someone else said, and you must know. You can be sure they believe they are doing you a favor and trying to help.

By getting involved in other people's problems, we get a rest from our race. It is easy to use their problems as an escape from our own. Just as I used to pretend, I was in a cooking show while in the kitchen. We want to make them believe we are Dr.Phil, and our advice will be the one thing that will change their lives and get us a trophy for a job well done.

Just like when you are in a bad traffic jam and when you approach the accident, suddenly realize that the people slowing down to look at the crash are making the situation worse. Either we cannot get enough drama in our race, or the fact that it is not happening to us makes it more appealing. We are wasting precious time in our limited race, pushing other people's cars instead of handling our own.

So how do we stop? We just do. We make the decision that we want to concentrate on our journey and leave the rest of the world alone. I say: "Not my cars," I keep going because that reminds me that I have enough cars to handle, so I do not need any extras. You will be busy with your own evasive maneuvers, trust me. When someone comes to you with advice, be as uninterested as possible. Just smile, nod, and tell them: "Thank you so much; I will consider it." I promise you they will stop. If they are looking for a reaction, not giving them one is the best way to guarantee it will stop. They might even get mad at you, and if they stop talking to you, you have one less thing to worry about.

If you want to drive the best race, do you want to waste time convincing others that they should be doing better in their race?

Why not take all that time and effort to understand finally:

What is the only thing that we can control?

Ourselves.

What is the only thing we can change?

The way we accept and embrace our race.

What is the only way we can do it?

One day at a time.

What do we need to keep our sanity throughout this race?

We need to balance our cars and put ourselves first.

How do we put ourselves first?

By taking bad drivers out of our journey.

How can we accept the detours on our road?

Looking at them as new possibilities.

How can we recover from our accidents?

Knowing that they make us stronger.

How do you survive a tornado on your road?

Learning to let go.

How do we take care of our car?

By taking care of ourselves.

Why do you need the best Pit Crew?

Because everyone needs reinforcements.

How do you learn to control your car?

By learning those evasive maneuvers.

When do we stop pushing other people's cars?

When we concentrate on our race.

I am not the only one who pushes when trying to open a door. When it does not work, I pull. We have the same problem in our race.

Want to know what I am talking about? Keep reading!

Chapter 11: Stop Pulling Other People's Cars

Enabler
1) One who helps something to happen.
2) One who encourages a bad habit in another by their behavior.
3) One who gives someone else the power to behave in a certain way.

We have car carriers and tow trucks, and then we have the ones that tie two cars together with a rope and pray all the way to their destination. They all have the same intention: to take a car that cannot or will not make a trip from point A to point B. We can produce a list of reasons a car needs to be pulled or transported during its life span. Some make more sense than others, but we do not need to justify it. If it is something that the owner of the car wants or needs to do, they try to decide the best way to go about it.

In the race of life, some cars are pulled down the road by others. The cars being pulled have a list of reasons to justify their situation. Some of the reasons might be:

-I did not ask you to bring me into this world, so it is your responsibility to take care of me.

-I do not have enough money.

-I can't find a job.

-I can't work for 40 hours a week.

-It is not my fault; it is the economy.

-I do not know what I want to do in life.

-I am still trying to find myself.

-I am waiting for the right opportunity.

On the other hand, the ones doing the pulling also have a list of excuses to justify their enabling. They will say:

-I feel guilty.

-What if something bad happens?

-It is only for a little while.

-It is for their own good.

-Blood is thicker than water.

-It is our responsibility.

-What will everyone say?

-It is impossible for them to make it on their own.

Again, if both cars in this equation are happy about the arrangement, we can all keep racing. However, suppose you are like thousands of other people tired of being responsible for someone else's cars, even when they are more than capable of driving their own. In that case, you should hear this: "It is not your job or your responsibility, and you must stop pulling them along during their race. You have your own cars to drive, and you are not a bad person if you let them learn their lessons. Even more, you are hurting them by taking away the opportunity for them to be the drivers in their race."

The part that I have witnessed many times in my own family is that the pulling of the cars is specific to which car they want you to pull. They might want you to pull their financial car but avoid getting involved in their relationship car; it's really convenient. These are not junker cars that cannot start or need parts. These are perfect cars that can have a successful race. Of course, it is easier to have someone else do the driving for them. However, it is on their terms, and you cannot tell them what to do.

Family and romantic relationships are the easier targets for this; we would not have this problem if we did not feel so guilty or if our emotions were not part of the equation. Our feelings betray us, making us an easy target for those who want to take advantage of our love. This situation is difficult to handle, and there is no easy formula to fix the problem. In this case, you do not get a happily ever after. When you cut the rope and stop pulling, you will probably lose the relationship with this person. They will likely be upset and offended that you finally realize their game and decide to put a stop to it. Eventually, they might understand what they did was wrong and return. However, that may never happen; you must be prepared for that.

The important thing here is to comprehend that we need to drive our cars in the race of life. Even if it breaks our hearts, we must use tough love and think about ourselves for a change. Our race will not last forever, and once you are not there for them anymore, they will need to learn how to drive on their own or look for another car to pull them along. Either way, it should not be your concern. You can let go.

Most of the time, you can hear parents, grandparents, and romantic partners complaining about someone taking advantage of their love for them. We love to sacrifice ourselves for others but will complain to everyone who listens. We will make sure everyone knows everything we are doing for others and how ungrateful they are at all we do for them. Again, it is like we are expecting some reward to become martyrs at the expense of our race.

If you tell them: "You know this is happening because you allow it. If you stop, you do not have to keep complaining and start taking charge of your race." Their answer every single time is: "Yes, I know, I should do that." So, why don't they do it? Because we are used to putting other people's needs before our own. We tend to care more about their race than our own, or we think that the purpose of our race is pulling their cars.

Here is an excellent opportunity to discuss the difference between helping and enabling. It is important to help one another in times of need. However, it is different when it becomes a habit or something expected of you. When saying: "No" or "I am sorry, but I can't right now" is not an option for you. Then you know it's not the help you are providing. You decide when and how you help others, which always makes you feel good about doing it. If it drains you and you feel like you can't say no, it's no longer help and becomes a problem.

Do not wait until you feel drained and used to understand:

What is the only thing that we can control?

Ourselves.

What is the only thing we can change?

The way we accept and embrace our race.

What is the only way we can do it?

One day at a time.

What do we need to keep our sanity throughout this race?

We need to balance our cars and put ourselves first.

How do we put ourselves first?

By taking bad drivers out of our journey.
How can we accept the detours on our road?
Looking at them as new possibilities.
How can we recover from our accidents?
Knowing that they make us stronger.
How do you survive a tornado on your road?
Learning to let go.
How do we take care of our car?
By taking care of ourselves.
Why do you need the best Pit Crew?
Because everyone needs reinforcements.
How do you learn to control your car?
By learning those evasive maneuvers.
When do we stop pushing other people's cars?
When we concentrate on our race.
When do we stop pulling other people's cars?
When we realize it is not our responsibility.

While pushing and pulling other people's cars will cause you to take your attention off the road and your race. We have one more distraction that can affect your journey.

Do you want to know what it is? Keep reading!

Chapter 12: Don't Judge Other People's Driving

Easier said than done, right?

We are 1,000 times better than Dr.Phil, remember?

"I can't believe she is wearing that."

"I'm sure he was married to someone else; that's not his wife."

"She doesn't make more money than me, so I wonder who got that for her?"

The truth is, we are clueless about everyone's race. Most of the time, we are clueless about our race. We turn everything into a competition to see who has the most significant problem or is more successful.

We like to escape our reality by looking at the car next door and saying:

"At least I'm not like them; I know better."

Life has a funny way to take you down a few pegs.

Let us say you are going down the road, there is a car riding next to you, and it has a dent, probably from a crash. Suddenly, you see that car cut another one while changing lanes. Think about what the first thing that comes to your mind will be. I will say: "No wonder the car is all messed up; look at how they drive." Then I realized I had no idea how the car got that dent. I assumed it was on the road, but maybe it was not. Perhaps the person driving the car now was not driving when the dent occurred. At the end of the day, why do I even care?

We love to judge other people; this is different from pushing their cars because at least people can argue that when they push other people's cars, they have good intentions or want to help, even if they do not. However, when judging others, we are ruthless and do not measure our comments or consequences.

I have another quote: "Before you judge someone, walk a mile in their shoes." You may have heard this saying or a variation of it. We know this is true deep inside, but we have a really challenging time minding our own business. What do we get from doing this? Your guess is as good as mine, but just as with any other habit, we can change it by putting the attention back on ourselves and our race.

We usually judge others against what is considered normal or what we believe is the correct opinion, behavior, or look. We have this need for control because, in our minds, it is the only way that we can be happy. The world will be perfect only when everyone thinks, acts, and looks the way it makes sense to you. It's annoying to us when people do things differently from how we think it's right, and they are happy. How dare they? It is not just fair they are happy when they feel and act in a way you think is not correct. You realize that's the reason you are not happy. So then, you decide it's time to convince everyone else you are right. We want them to change and do things the way we want because we know it is the right way. We are sure that if we all think, act, and look the same way, the world will be perfect, and as a result, your life will finally be how you want it to be. You will be happy if everyone else changes to make your life better. The truth is the race of life doesn't work that way, but the fascinating part is that you don't need everyone else to think or agree with you to be happy. Now that's a game changer, very liberating.

That is why I have never been a fan of the one-size-fits-all solutions. Unless you consider each person's uniqueness, trying to fit everyone into the same mold is impossible. For example, not all relationships are equal. When two people decide to be together, they must determine their own rules about how they will work together as a couple. It only needs to work for them when other people see their relationship and say: "I couldn't live like that; I don't know why they do that." Guess what? You don't have to do it because it is not your relationship. You don't need to know why they do it because it is not your problem. If we practice the philosophy of "to each their own," we can all get along much better.

Sadly, many people out there make a lot of money and hold a lot of power because they are good at convincing us that our problems are someone else's fault. They do not want you to know that you are in control of your car and that it does not matter what other cars do along the way. You can be happy if you are focused on your race. These people derive their power from us giving our power away. How do they do it? They try to change a race that is supposed to be independent, and they put us in groups. They also want every group to try to change the other group's minds.

So, we are riding down the road and trying to make the best of our journey. Then, these people tell you that you need to pick a group because there is power in numbers, and if we ride together, we can have a better race. Then they ask you to take the other groups off the road so we can have a better journey. Now, the problem is that you start looking for your group. You think you found the one that fits you best, but then you realize some of the drivers in that group have other ideas different from yours, and you don't fit there either. So, you continue your drive and try to find a group that will suit you, and you know what we find out at the end? We will not find a group that can fit all our beliefs because we are all unique and have different opinions. We all feel like something is wrong with us and end up fighting with everyone we meet. On our road, instead of having a race where everyone is moving forward and carefree down the highway, we have the most ridiculous pile-up ever. Many cars are trying to go this way and that way, thinking they have to fit in and choose a group.

I finally understood this message after years of being on social media. I was one of the people who was convinced that the world would be a better place if we could all agree on the same things. Honestly, I have no idea how I let myself be brainwashed like that when I knew that even in our own family, we could not agree on what restaurant to eat in when going out. How could billions of people agree to anything? Trying to get everyone to agree is not the solution to all the world's problems, but we love to fit a square into a hole, so we keep doing it. During that time, I was riding a daily roller-coaster of emotions that was not doing me any good. Then, when my daughter's divorce came along, we decided to close all our accounts until things got resolved and talk about relief. Suddenly, problems and discussions disappeared, my world became peaceful, and I loved it. Also, I realized that my life went on; even if I did not know everything happening or the latest reason, we all needed to be outraged.

Once I stopped spending time on social media, I had more free time to work on myself and my family. I did not have the excuse that I did not have the time anymore. I started with my house. I wanted to take my house back, and that is exactly what I did. I went to YouTube and found Dawn (The Minimal Mom), Cas (Clutterbug), and Dana (A Slob Comes Clean). I binge-watched their videos about minimalism, organizing, and decluttering and went to work. Later, I found out they had a course, Take your House Back, "how fitting," I thought, and I took it. Together with these amazing ladies, I was able to take back control of my house and my life. I hope, someday, I can let them know that I will be forever grateful for their help during this challenging time. While working in my house, I knew I needed to work on my feelings and try to understand everything I was going through. So, I returned to YouTube and found two excellent channels: Wu Wei Wisdom with therapist David James Lees and Narcdaily with Andrew. These two great men were able to help me find peace and clarity at a time when I was feeling lost. They are all part of my crew, and I am incredibly grateful.

It took me two years to go through this transition, and now I feel like a completely different person. I decided to stop judging others because:

1. I do not have time for that anymore. I am working on myself.
2. I realized everyone is different.
3. Each of us is going through our journey.
4. I do not need anyone to change for me to be happy.

So, I hope that you can also understand:

What is the only thing that we can control?

Ourselves.

What is the only thing we can change?

The way we accept and embrace our race.

What is the only way we can do it?

One day at a time.

What do we need to keep our sanity throughout this race?

We need to balance our cars and put ourselves first.

How do we put ourselves first?

By taking bad drivers out of our journey.

How can we accept the detours on our road?

Looking at them as new possibilities.

How can we recover from our accidents?

Knowing that they make us stronger.

How do you survive a tornado on your road?

Learning to let go.

How do we take care of our car?

By taking care of ourselves.

Why do you need the best Pit Crew?

Because everyone needs reinforcements.
How do you learn to control your car?
By learning those evasive maneuvers.
When do we stop pushing other people's cars?
When we concentrate on our race.
When do we stop pulling other people's cars?
When we realize it is not our responsibility.
Why don't we need to judge others?
Because their life is not our problem.
We have come far; how are you feeling?
Ready for the final lap? Keep reading.

Part 5: The Final Lap

Chapter 13: The Finish Line

The end of the race is a mystery to all of us.
Sometimes, we wish to know when that moment will come to prepare ourselves. We want to leave everything ready and end the race with a bang.
Others wish to end the race fast, and without noticing, it ends. Just keep driving into the sunset without looking back.
All of us are terrified of that moment and how others will remember our race after we are gone.
Newsflash: you are not in control of that either.

The last quote of the book: "All good things must come to an end." It does not matter if you finish your race full speed ahead or need a push past the finish line; the end comes for all of us. Regardless of what your personal beliefs are about the afterlife. I think we can all agree that, in the end, we want to be able to say: "I was happy." Again, the definition of happiness is very personal, and I hope that after reading this book, you understand that it comes from you. Many things can bring you happiness, but you cannot be genuinely happy unless you look within.

I worked at a funeral home as an office administrator for two and a half years. That meant I was the first contact everyone had when calling or visiting the funeral home. I worked with families, hospitals, nursing homes, hospices, and medical examiners. Also, I contacted the doctors, state, and health department to acquire the death certificate. Plus, I did the service's DVDs, signature books, and prayer cards. Each task was as different as the families we were privileged to serve during a difficult time.

When people asked me where I worked, and I told them I worked at a funeral home, their reaction was priceless. They would open their eyes wide and say: "Oh my God, I could never do that." "Don't you get scared?" Then very slowly, they would take a step back away from me like I had the death cooties. I found it amusing. The truth is that my job revolved more around the families than their loved ones, and each situation was as different as the person who passed away. It was never dull, that is for sure.

I met the people who came to do their pre-arrangements because they wanted to make sure everything was in order when their time came. Also, the families that visited us when their loved one was in the hospital facing imminent death, to the ones who had to face unexpected tragedies. I learned one thing: at the end of our race, we do not have any control over how we will be remembered by the ones left behind. We cannot control their grief or their apathy. The decisions on the arrangements made will not make any difference to us. I am sure we will not care about how many people show up, and I know none of us would appreciate the family drama during that time.

If I could choose one thing as my favorite part of the job, it would be doing the DVDs. That's when I got a glimpse of the person we were honoring. If the family brought the pictures, they would share the stories about them. I understood that the journey during our race was what truly mattered. In this part, I will admit that I did talk to them while fixing the chapel or arranging the flowers. You will be glad to know that they never answered back.

If you have experienced a time when you were close to death, I am sure you can agree with the fact that there is nothing we can do about it. During my last pregnancy, I was 37 years old. It was quite a different experience from my first two, and I suffered from pre-eclampsia postpartum. My daughter was only five days old when my husband had to drive me back to the hospital because I was having trouble breathing. As soon as I got there, I was rushed in, and for 5 hours, I had multiple doctors trying to stabilize me. I was not in control of my body. What I did didn't matter; I couldn't bring my blood pressure down. I remember when the doctor told my husband: "If this doesn't work, we have to take her to the ICU." I had a newborn baby at home, and I didn't know if I could make it. Thankfully, they were able to stabilize me and took 6 liters of liquid from my body. I lost 30 pounds of liquid in 3 days, so you can imagine how swollen I've gotten. To this day, they have no idea what happened, but I know it changed how I saw my life and how quickly things can go south.

Having the experience to work daily around death helps you appreciate every day gifted to you. Every time I saw a mother crying over the loss of one of their children, it made me realize how blessed I am to have my kids. When we were faced with the possibility of losing our grandchild, it made us face the reality of how fragile life truly is and not take any moment for granted. We are on this fantastic planet for a while, so let us make the best of this experience. Let us decide today to drive in this race of life with a purpose, to live every day like it is the last, and we will let everyone else in our lives do the same.

It was my honor to share my life experiences so far with you.
I hope that this book blessed you.
I wish you could use it to find the peace and happiness we crave.

If someday we see each other on this journey, I will ask you, "Are you moving your cars?"

I WILL LEAVE THIS HERE for you one last time, so you do not forget:

What is the only thing that we can control?
Ourselves.
What is the only thing we can change?
The way we accept and embrace our race.
What is the only way we can do it?
One day at a time.
What do we need to keep our sanity throughout this race?
We need to balance our cars and put ourselves first.
How do we put ourselves first?
By taking bad drivers out of our journey.
How can we accept the detours on our road?
Looking at them as new possibilities.
How can we recover from our accidents?
Knowing that they make us stronger.
How do you survive a tornado on your road?
Learning to let go.
How do we take care of our car?
By taking care of ourselves.
Why do you need the best Pit Crew?
Because everyone needs reinforcements.
How do you learn to control your car?
By learning those evasive maneuvers.

When do we stop pushing other people's cars?

When we concentrate on our race.

When do we stop pulling other people's cars?

When we realize it is not our responsibility.

Why don't we need to judge others?

Because their life is not our problem.

What is important in our final lap?

If you were happy during your race.

Have the best time driving your car, enjoying the road, and appreciating your journey!

Love,

Nitza

P.S.

If you want to apply these lessons to your own race, get a notebook and keep reading. I will provide a list of tasks you can do to make sure your race is a great one.

Part 6: Apply the Lessons

For this part all you need is a pen and paper.
You can use a journal, notebook or lose paper.
Have fun!

Hello again:

    I am so happy that you want to feel better and learn how to drive in your race.

I hope you enjoyed the book and now is the time to put those lessons to work.

Since each race is different, I made this part for you to apply all the chapters to your reality.

Follow these steps so you can learn about yourself, your cars, your race, and hopefully what you need to do to have a better journey.

Have the best time driving your car, enjoying the road, and appreciating your journey!

Love,

Nitza

Chapter 1: Accepting your Car

Are you ready to accept your car?

This is your first task.

I want you to draw multiple hearts and write on each one a unique thing about yourself, from your appearance to your attributes and skills. Even if you find something you don't particularly like, if it is part of your car, write it. Feel free to draw as many hearts as you will need to make sure you get to know and accept yourself for the amazing and unique person that you are.

Now, after you have filled out all your hearts, write down how you feel about yourself on the next page. Please be honest; you can burn it after you finish. You must accept your car, which means you must face your feelings. That way, you can work on changing thoughts slowing down your race.

Chapter 2: Balancing Your Cars

Now is the time to balance your cars.

On another page, you are going to draw some rectangles. Each one is going to represent a car that you drive. Please write all the different categories you are driving. Remember, if you have a car for your family, write family. However, if it's more specific, like brother or mother, write down precisely what you are dealing with. In other words, write everything that takes up part of your time, your day, or your mind here so you can face everything you are trying to balance in your race.

Good job! Can you see why you are so exhausted? That's a lot of cars. On the next page, you will make a stand and choose the cars you will drive. Remember to put yourself first. Look and identify all the cars you are driving that are not yours and plan how to get those out of your race. Return some cars to their rightful owners and get your race to a more manageable pace. If you are asking too much of yourself, maybe you need to put some cars in a garage for a while, and you can take them out again when you feel ready.

The goal is to balance your race so you can feel happy about your journey instead of overwhelmed.

Chapter 3: Good Drivers, Bad Drivers

I hope you feel more in control after making a plan to balance your cars. In this part, you are going to identify the bad drivers on your journey. Be very honest about who they are and why they are bad for your race. I understand that sometimes they can't just disappear out of your race; however, if you know who they are, you can protect yourself from them. Then, you will write yourself an insurance policy on how you will deal with these drivers. If you can keep them out of your race, that's perfect. If that is not possible, write some strategies that feel comfortable for you on how you will protect your car against them. Have fun! Write the best insurance policy that you can; it's free.

Chapter 4: Detours

This part will allow you to find a detour in your life. Remember that a detour is anything that makes you change your plans and go in a different direction. I want you to write about the detour and what happened. Then, please write about the changes it brought to your race. Lastly, I was hoping you could write about how that detour was good for you. I want you to see that every detour in your life brings some type of change and that it can be good for you if you embrace it.

Chapter 5: Accidents on the Road

Now, you get to write about an accident in your race. The accident can be something that happened to you personally or to someone in your life and that changed the circumstances of your race. Please describe what happened and how it affected you. Then, please write what you learned from this experience and how it strengthened you.

Chapter 6: The Tornado on the Road

In this part, you can write about a tornado in your race. If you can't think of one experience that you can qualify as a tornado, go to the next chapter. If you have faced a tornado, I want you to write about the experience and how it affected you.

Then, could you write about letting it go?

It will be a process, and it will take time, but it is important that you forgive yourself for your role in this storm and that you let go of resentment toward others involved.

It will bring you peace, and I want that for you.

Chapter 7: Stop for Gas

Now is the time for some pampering.
Please write down at least three things you can do to care for yourself.
Think about three for your physical health, three for your mental
health, and three for your spiritual health.
Then, I want you to write a promise to yourself, explaining all these
things that you will do because you deserve it. Make a plan on how you
are going to incorporate them one at a time into your week and start
looking forward to some love and caring. Even if you decide to buy
yourself some flowers every week, take a bubble bath, or have some
quiet time, the point is to get used to the idea that it is okay for you to
care about yourself.

Chapter 8: Pit Stop

Ready to identify your Pit Crew?
I want you to write about all the people on your team. Write their names and why you want them on your crew. Remember, this list can change, and feel free to adjust all the members of your team depending on their performance. Please keep in mind that they are in your race to support you, not to drive your race for you.

Chapter 9: The Owner's Manual

This next part is a way to write down everything that works for you, your owner's manual. Take this time to think about what works for you. Remember, don't compare yourself with anyone else, and don't try to justify why you think, feel, or act that way. This task allows you to get to know yourself, the real you, not the one other people want to see. For example: Do I like to eat my food really hot? or Do I like to wait until my food gets cold to eat it?
Choose the things that work for you and know they are just right.

Chapter 10: Stop Pushing Other People's Cars

Are you ready to look at yourself and be honest about who you are pushing during this race?

We are not assigning blame here; this is a way for you to face the truth about a part of your race that can be lighter.

During Chapter 2, did you realize that some of those cars were not yours?

Please make a list of all the cars you are pushing for others in your life and then decide to start giving them back.

Let's start saying: "Not my cars."

Chapter 11: Stop Pulling Other People's Cars

You know what I'm going to say here. Let's make a list of all the people you are pulling during your race and the reasons why you are pulling them. Then, it will be your pleasure to stop doing it because you have your own cars to drive.

Let's say it again: "Not my cars."

You are getting it.

Chapter 12: Don't Judge Other People's Driving

I know that you never do this, but if you can humor me, make a list of reasons why we usually judge people. It can be because of how they look, act, or talk; even their job can be a reason why we judge them. Then, at the end, please write in big letters: None of these are my problems because they're not my cars!

Now, doesn't that feel so much better?

Chapter 13: The Finish Line

Congratulations! You did all the work.
How are you feeling?
Ready for the finish line.
This next task is going to be fun; I promise.
I want you to write a bucket list.
Now that you have more time to do the things that make you happy,
write a list and start working on everything you want to do.
Have fun and take it one day at a time!

Don't miss out!

Visit the website below and you can sign up to receive emails whenever Nitza Haydee Caro publishes a new book. There's no charge and no obligation.

https://books2read.com/r/B-A-UZCFB-UTSZC

BOOKS 2 READ

Connecting independent readers to independent writers.

www.ingramcontent.com/pod-product-compliance
Lightning Source LLC
Chambersburg PA
CBHW031439130726
47989CB00003B/1208